The Elephant

for Leah

This book has been reviewed
for accuracy by

Merlin D. Tuttle, Ph.D.
Curator of Mammals
Milwaukee Public Museum

Library of Congress Number: 79-13307

6 7 8 9 10 11 12 13 14   W   99 98 97 96 95 94 93 92

Library of Congress Cataloging in Publication Data

Hogan, Paula Z
   The elephant.

   Cover title: The life cycle of the elephant.
   SUMMARY: Describes in simple terms the life cycle
of the elephant.
   1. Elephants—Juvenile literature.   [1. Elephants]
I. Craft, Kinuko.   II. Title.   III. Title: The
life cycle of the elephant.
QL737.P98H6   599'.61   79-13307
ISBN 0-8172-1505-0   hardcover library binding
ISBN 0-8114-8177-8   softcover binding

The
ELEPHANT

By Paula Z. Hogan
Illustrations by Kinuko Craft

RSVP
RAINTREE
STECK-VAUGHN
PUBLISHERS
The Steck-Vaughn Company

 # The Elephant

Elephants eat almost all day long. They are the largest animals on land. Even their babies weigh more than a full-grown man.

A newborn elephant tries to walk right after birth. At first it trips and falls. Two days later a baby can keep up with the adults.

The mother elephant gives milk to her baby. She must watch it carefully. Lions might hunt for small elephants.

9

Baby elephants are always in trouble. They have play fights and climb over grown-ups. Sometimes they get stuck in the mud.

Several elephants live in a herd. All the adults help care for the baby. An older female leads the herd.

The leader looks out for danger.
If lions are near she moves her
herd away. At times she attacks
the lions.

Elephants are very friendly. They greet each other by touching with their trunks. Herds sometimes join together.

Young elephants must learn to drink with their trunks. They suck up water and pour it into their mouths.

When they are about two years old, young elephants begin to grow tusks. They can use tusks to push down trees. That's how elephants eat leaves from the highest branches.

On hot days elephants rest in the shade. They keep cool by spraying water on their backs.

Female elephants never leave the herd. They stay with their mothers and sisters. Each female has one best friend.

After reaching the age of twelve,
most male elephants live alone.
Once in a while they visit the herd
to mate with females.

Elephants live about sixty years.
As elephants grow older, their
teeth wear down. Old elephants
sometimes die because they
cannot eat.

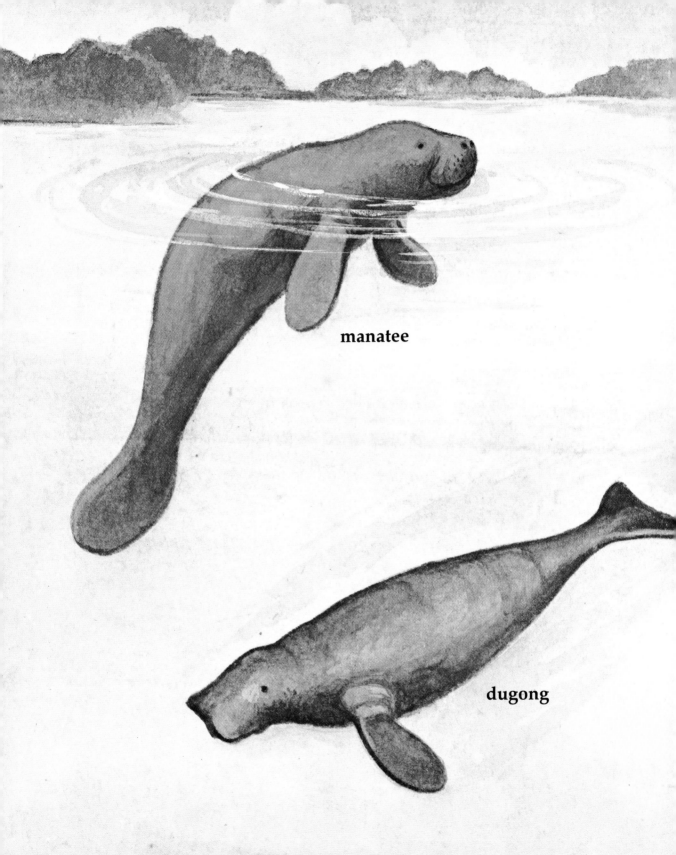

manatee

dugong

hyrax

Some of the elephant's nearest relatives lead very different lives. Hyraxes are small and covered with fur. Dugongs and manatees live underwater. None share the elephant's trunk or great size.

GLOSSARY

These words are explained the way they are used in this book. Words of more than one syllable are in parentheses. The heavy type shows which syllable is stressed.

attack (at·**tack**) — to fight against

dugong (**du**·gong) — underwater animal that is a relative of the elephant

full-grown — having grown up to become an adult

greet — to say hello

herd — a group of elephants

hyrax (**hy**·rax) — small, furry relative of the elephant

lion (**li**·on) — large, strong cat that hunts elephants

manatee (**man**·a·tee) — underwater animal like a dugong, with a bigger tail

newborn (**new**·born) — just born

relative (**rel**·a·tive) — related to another animal

spraying (**spray**·ing) — blowing water in small drops

suck — to draw water in through the trunk

trunk — an elephant's long snout

tusks — long teeth that stick out of an elephant's mouth